Prison Guide
Prison Survival Secrets Revealed

2012 Edition

By

A Pisano

Friends,

I believe the essential survival skills that I had to learn the hard way should be shared, and not held as secrets to use against the naive, and unsuspecting "new Jacks" entering the prison system.

The secrets of prison survival have been unwritten for decades and countless people have suffered.

It was obvious that there was a need for this book, in which reveals this critical information. Feelings of anxiety and helplessness flood the mind of the inexperienced inmate. I believe that preparation and guidance is the best approach to be ready for the sudden lifestyle change that comes with being imprisoned.

The fact is that nobody gives you what I offer because nobody has my experience. I am a true veteran and you will be hard pressed to find anyone that is willing to share with you what I know.

This guide has been written collectively over the course of ten years and contains the lessons that the hardened veterans follow.

Prison Guide: Prison Survival Secrets Revealed is compact with all content, no filler, and no sequel.

Enjoy,

A. Pisano

Contents

Introduction

This is a serious book; it's not for everyone. What I am about to reveal is straight up serious business and this book is the truth. The content may conflict with the values of some individuals but that is what it takes to survive in such a drastically different place. It is Prison.

The behavior and psychology revealed in this book are the collective work of many people, and comprised to be proven effective for anyone. Through many years of research and development, trial and error, I have observed, studied and collected the systems of veterans. The documented secrets are geared toward the inmate looking to go home on his earliest release date.

I have practiced the survival tactics myself and have over ten years' experience in the prison system. It will be easy for anyone to apply these survival methods if you are open and willing to put forth effort.

PART ONE: Survival Action & Inaction

5 Ways to Be Prepared and Ready NOW

You are preparing for your first day of jail. You're going through changes, feelings of loneliness, rejection, fear, and hopelessness. The inevitable doom of going to prison is arriving and you feel you can't do anything about it, right?

That is wrong. You still have the power and control, and you are about to make a commitment that will give you clarity through this cloudy stage. You are going to need some education and guidance to show you that you *do* have power, but rest assured, you are still in control. Everyone needs education and guidance, and that's okay. It's important to know where you're at, what you need to proceed, accept where you're going, and move on. You can only control yourself, right? So let's get into what you can do to prepare yourself *now*, so you can be ready for the volatile world that is prison.

I. Don't Look For Friends

Prison is unlike any other environment. It's comparable to landing in a foreign country, as it *is* a foreign place to millions of people and it should be respected as such. Imagine a caged facility where you don't know any of the locals, don't speak the language, and are constantly under harsh scrutiny about the things that you cannot change about yourself. Imagine it's your first day in jail and you don't even know anything about the people, or the place. You might think its ok to meet new people here, but believe me; these people do **not** want your friendship. You abandoned your friends in your old country and you are now somewhere new, far away.

You can no longer get back to your home life until you survive where you're at in the present. As a matter of fact, you are going to have to *forget* your prior life, and that you even *had* any friends prior to coming here if you even *hope* to make it out of here safely. So, from here on in, you're completely on your own, so it's best you detach from the past.

When you walk inside for the first time, keep your head down. Do not actively search for a potential friend.

If you're looking left and right you're viewed as wimpy and searching for a friend to help you. These people **do not want** to be your friend. Walk straight to where you are going with conviction. Let them watch you if they wish. So what? You will walk with full confidence and strength and not like a coward looking for an aid. The snakes slither closely and will sense any fear and strike before you ever know what happened.

II. They are Sizing You Up: Body Language

You are different; there is no denying that the locals are stalking you, praying to see a glimpse of weakness; the place is rampant with anger, affliction and neglect in every direction. Sometimes, in this environment, it may *appear* to be tolerable because people need to eat and conduct their daily activities, but make no mistake about it; you *are* being sized up, the "new guy."

A. The Size Up

'Sizing you up' means to appraise you, to search you critically in very fine detail. They are looking to get an idea of your body type, your personality, and your intelligence. This is for many reasons: curiosity, their own protection, checking you out to be a potential target for a robbery, extortion, or competition in general. It varies why people size you up. Either way, you do not know anyone's prior history or intentions; so just know that you are being watched. Logically, Inmates do it to be aware of who is around at all times.

Stop smiling; stop smirking. Don't nervously touch your face. Stand tall and walk in full confidence with a blank expression, or even an angry look on your face. That's exactly how you should be feeling, right?

This isn't a game. This is prison. A place where you really don't want to be, so you had better wake up and pay close attention to what you're doing if you want to walk out of here unscathed. Get that smirk off your face because in here, **YOU** are **NOT** the tough guy. In your world, you may have been someone special, but not here.

In prison, the saying goes: "You have only three options on how you leave this place: A man, a fag, or in a body bag." *You* better be the one choosing. I suggest you choose quickly before someone else decides for you, because the people you're walking amongst are going to try to put you into the one category that best suits *them*. Who cares about *you*? You're the new face that the inmates see as a number.

III. Foreign Environment: Look & Observe

The thousands of pounds of cold steel bars surround you, and you can literally feel tension in the air as sharp as the razor wire that wraps the perimeter of the compound. The cold steel acts as a symbolic weight dragging you down into the negativity seeping below. This isn't a game, this is real life and you're alone with no one to help, so causing any problems, would not be a good idea.

Horror, agitation, and despair that you can't even imagine call this place home. There are many things happening behind the scoured walls of this place that you don't even want to know about. There are partnerships, cults, gangs, and sects of thugs here with long histories. There are also deep rivalries with severe friction. Anyone wearing an opposing color to their preference has only one option. For the opposition, it can only be death. There are such dreadful tensions, race wars, and political revolutions brewing; you don't even know where to be, or what not to do. This place could be only a few miles from your home, but be sure, this is nothing like your neighborhood. You are completely off the map and the perimeter surrounding this compound keeps you locked inside this micro-community. And anything you're familiar with is locked out so to get back to *your* neighborhood, you're going to have to familiar with *this* neighborhood.

Your pampered world still has a scent on you and it makes the locals sick. Get rid of your normal habits because in this environment, you had better observe more, talk less, and think faster. Do you think you're going to just pass through the heartless penitentiary with the smell of a girl's sweet perfume all over you? These are the toughest, coldest convicts of your state and you already have a look that screams target, as you are the new face on the block. You had better change your outlook and observe everyone and everything around you. Listen for who is loud and obnoxious so you can have an idea who is best to avoid.

Listen for people that add respect in their tone when they speak to others and take mental notes. Look to see who is cleaning the place and who is taking care of themselves to get an idea of who is who in the new environment.

Generally, the "A-man" gives and receives a lot of respect to/from the other inmates. The A-man usually has top seniority in the housing unit and is viewed by staff as following the rules. He is in a position of authority and simply observing those in powerful positions, usually those with the most seniority, will give you great insight as to what is expected and favorable in the environment.

Don't talk much, but if you do, always be sure to speak politely, with manners and respect, because the villains in this environment don't care about you. Everything you say or do will have a response so stay mindful of the reactions you provoke. Everyone is there by force, and not by choice.

In your first few days and in general, keep strangers at a distance. You obviously don't know who is who, and you don't want to get caught up or identified associating with the wrong person or people. There will come a time when you do have associates, but, before you start to open any lines of communication, you should have a feeling of who is who. Keep your goals of returning to your family close to you because it is very easy to get side tracked into things that are not important, so be vigilant about going home daily.

Move very slowly with everything you do. Consider all the possibilities of your actions and the how certain outcomes may have unexpected consequences. So take time to stop and think, watch others, smell the areas around, and listen for potential threats. They may not come, but being prepared is way better than not, so use all your senses to guide you through the complex maze that is prison. Do what is most important to survive this place and what the other veterans are doing: *observe.*

IV. Keep Doors Closed and Keep Your Distance

Being the new face, you will be confronted daily by people that will try you. Some are simply bored and want conversation, some will taunt, some are sizing you up, and some are already searching to get something from you. They are seeking a reaction, information, food, cigarettes, or just about anything, really. **Your best bet in this cold environment is to say nothing to anyone because the more you engage, the more you reveal about yourself.** The more you talk, the more you teach. It's advisable to be silent until you have been there long enough to really learn about the environment. Like I said, people will *try* to converse with you, but you don't *have to* respond. Its better you don't respond when people try to open doors with you. Once you open doors to you, there's very little chance of ever closing them again.

A. Opening a Door

'Opening a door' means opening lines of communication, which is an opportunity to become familiar. Those who wouldn't normally talk to you, now try to familiarize themselves with you. This may be a simple question, a joke, an insult or even a friendly gesture. If someone is trying to open a door with you for no apparent reason, they usually have ulterior motives. Do you really think they just want to be friends? It's usually an attempt by those in need to use you for food and goods to support them.

Another term for this is "friendly extortion." They will constantly ask for things of value using the fake ploy of friendship as leverage.

This familiarity is something you don't want, as it's interpreted as freedom of access to you and your possessions. Further, once doors are open, it's nearly impossible to close them as certain inmates won't stop pestering you. If you allow this to happen, there will be people lining up to take advantage of you.

A potential enemy wants to keep that door open for as long as he can to extort you, swindle you, and coerce you into things. So keep the door closed with everyone, by avoiding everyone, until *you* are ready to move on *your terms*.

V.Alliances: How & When to Connect

In prison, it is okay to make alliances, even necessary at times, but you must know a few key rules before you reach out to anyone.

You must observe *before* you move. Don't dare talk to people the first day you're there. Or even the second day.

If you're comfortable, break the ice on the third day. Start with shallow conversation, common ground, and no more. Do not dump your problems, as everyone there has tons of problems. Do not ask for anything. Simply discuss something in common that's present at that moment. Usually, in small doses, humor works. Remember, if you talk too much, too soon, you risk opening up so many doors with people, it will be impossible to close them all. But it is safe to make alliances. You must be cautious, patient, and observant when making a connection with a possible associate.

You never know who you're dealing with in this place. An inmate could have a lot friction in the jail, and his enemies will attack you just as they would attack him. Your potential ally could be a serial child rapist, and you may not know until you suffer the consequences. Guilty by association is profound in jail so be careful. It's always best to observe as much as you can, listen, and make decisions very, **very** slowly.

You are not going anywhere and, like I said, if you start opening the wrong doors with people, it is equivalent to starting unnecessary problems for yourself. **It's always safer to err on the side of solitude, than it is to invite bad company.**

Maybe This Isn't For You

In all fairness, if you're happy from what you've been getting out of life, then by all means, keep on doing what you're doing.

If you're confident you have all the answers then don't bother to read further. Put the book down, as you "know" what you're doing. Arrogance will get you hurt, but don't take my word for it. I have only ten years working as a master of prison survival.

Maybe you don't want the information from *me*, and that's ok, but you should still get the information. Maybe your plans are better? But if being sized up and stalked like prey is not for you, there are lessons that can help you avoid the traps.

You are not hopeless, *if*, you are open to looking at new information and learning the survival secrets. So before you really mess up and invite all kinds of problems for yourself, I suggest you pay attention to the *current* approaches.

Veterans in prison that know survival methods deliberately keep the secrets for themselves, so they can **use them on you**, the new inmate. I suggest you listen like you've never listened before because the secrets I am about to share have been handed down for decades to get here.

I give you what stone-cold prison veterans **should be** telling the new guys coming in from the streets. The experienced veterans don't teach the youth today because they either want to use your ignorance against you for their gain, or because new inmates are too arrogant and stubborn to simply listen to good direction.

Remember: a man, a fag, or a body bag. Straight up!

7 Secrets to Survive Prison

I. Shut Up Sometimes

Talk minimally. Period!

If you just observe, keep to yourself, and are patient, all the questions you may have *will be* answered, so speak less than the average person. Don't ask questions. Don't be curious. Any answer that you need, like when to eat, call someone, or handle something will be provided to you. Upon reception, you need time to process if you are compatible with the local prisoners, and they need time to observe you as well. Wait at least a few days before starting a conversation, and although this may sound isolating, it's exactly what this environment is, confinement.

Your thoughts are your own business, so feel free to think what you want, but be sure to keep them to yourself. Further, do you *really* want to get familiar with the locals? Think about it. Although there are positive stand-up associates to be made in jail, the fact is, they can *never* compensate for your family. So, if you care to bond, its best you save your intimate conversations for the visits, phone calls, and letters for the people who you care about. More importantly, for those who care about *you.*

In this place nobody cares about you, as people are there by force, and not by choice. Countless people have entered prison and have created trouble for themselves without even knowing how they did it. Most think they know what they are walking into and quickly find out just how wrong it can be to assume they know the intricate dynamics.

There are numerous personality types throughout prison and unsuspecting inmates are quickly recognized as being new to the environment. **You should consider that the communication in jail is swift, quick and absolute.**

People in other housing locations will know what you do or say shortly after you do or say it, as the veterans are always watching and listening. The most crucial secret for survival is to simply be quiet and that's why its number one.

You don't have to speak even when you normally would outside of prison. If someone asks you a dumb question or anything for that matter, say nothing. Don't even acknowledge them. You don't owe anybody anything and you entered jail alone. You are not obligated to explain a single thing to a single person at any time and if someone were to demand anything from you, even conversation, they would be out of line, so keep in mind that you dictate your engagements, not anybody else. By maintaining your position and standing your ground, you will clearly establish you have rigid standards and are not weak.

There will be times when people will test you, probe you and try to get you to reveal something, anything. If you just shut up, they will take that as a sign of power and control. More importantly, they have no idea what you are thinking, and will likely stop bothering you. If someone tries to joke on you, call you out, or say something bad about you, simply disregard as if you never heard it. You just ignore it because veterans know: "He is not talking about me. He is nobody important in my life and I am not even going to acknowledge him." An attitude like this lets everyone around know that you must have serious issues on your mind if you are not even reacting to them. It will have a stronger effect than any response you could come up with to counter them.

Generally, inmates inevitably get social with each other from being confined together so long and sometimes the familiarity breeds disrespect because people get too comfortable. But you can control that by keeping your own attitude and actions in control. Even if some asks you a simple question: "Where are you from?" "How did you get that?" you can simply say nothing if you aren't comfortable revealing information. It's always better to err on the side of being rude and silent than polite and talkative.

II. Mind Your Business

The importance of this cannot be stressed enough. You have to live amongst the surrounding inmates, and there's no escape, so keep your focus on what *you* should be doing: **Your own time.**

When everyone else has an opinion on things, keep your comments to yourself, and people will respect you for knowing your boundaries. Even a simple slip of your words can have repercussions so just be in tune to where you are, who is around, and what you need to be doing for yourself.

Things can heat up quickly, even if you're only trying to help, but if you are constantly minding your own business, even when others aren't, you'll clearly establish credibility that shows you know when to stay out of the affairs of other people.

There may come a time when you are asked for your opinion on another inmate. It is always best to keep your opinions to yourself, whether good or bad, and simply say you're focusing on your own issues. You don't know all the alliances around, and even if things seem obvious, people constantly change. Someone who you think may be an ally today could possibly be a source of tension the next day.

Obviously you have some legal issues to work out and that is the reason why you are incarcerated. To get involved with the community gossip is a sure way into trouble and if you're trying to survive, you should keep your opinions on your own situation and keep a boundary line about *your* life. Your case is what is keeping you imprisoned. Are you going to the law library to research any mitigating factors? Jail offers a means to empower yourself if you utilize the time wisely and if mind your own affairs, you can add to your own growth and development. The people around are not as interesting or important as you. Keep to your own concerns; your case, family, and affairs.

Don't comment on someone else's mail, visits, packages, phone calls, or anything for that matter. That's entirely their business and getting involved with someone else is something you cannot easily back out of because once the door is open, it cannot be easily closed. Don't even look at what they are doing. Don't have any interest in other people's affairs at all. If something goes down, keep reading, writing or whatever you were in the middle of doing at the time. Obviously, if something is directly going to affect you, you should be aware that something is occurring. But when it comes to other people, if you get into something that is not your business, it may become your business and now your problem. You would inherit them and their problems into your life. Remember, you can never take back anything you say and do.

People don't really get into trouble for being too quiet or staying to themselves. But I know countless people that have gotten into serious trouble, life threatening trouble, for talking too much about other people's matters. That's why it is very important to be very mindful of all you say and do.

A. Non-Verbal

Be sure to be strict with your non-verbal communication as well. For instance, if you witness a fight, don't be part of the crowd that turns to stare, as everyone facing the same direction will definitely alert the guard's interest. Once the guards get involved, people get into trouble.

Further, getting other inmates into trouble can make you become a target as well. Some prisoners actively search for other inmates who attract the officer's attention to make them a target. It can happen quickly, so be aware of what you're doing.

Some inmates choose to have a constant look of discomfort on their faces as a defense mechanism to keep others away. This is an effective method as others interpret your discomfort as normal in the prison environment. And they, like you, don't want to incur any more problems than they already have, so if you *appear* to have an ill-adjusted attitude then it can be viewed as a clear sign to stay away.

Steer clear of being offensive as to avoid provoking a problem, but those that make it clear that they are not an easily approachable socialite have been known to keep others away.

B. Mind Your Property

If something doesn't belong to you, **do not** touch it. Stealing is a sure way into dangerous territory. Nobody likes a "sneak thief" because all the inmates live together, and are vulnerable to each other. Anyone can get their personals taken, and it's not respectable when people do it.

Of course, it does happen, but it's viewed as taking advantage and abusive, and the majority of prisoners don't respect thievery.

Keep in mind, a theft that's upfront and in your presence is a completely different type of robbery, and we'll cover how to avoid that later. Many people live by codes that call for violence as soon as their property is taken.

If you're trying to survive prison and not get into a sure swift bout of jailhouse violence, then keep your hands to yourself and don't take what doesn't belong to you.

III. Gangs

Some people value climbing to the top of their gang's "set" and if that is your interest, then maybe this book isn't for you. Again, this is for the reader seeking to make decisions based on going home, *to stay.*

Of course, many gangs offer their members an intimate community in which the dynamics are familial and it is reasonable why some would chose gang life, as some can appreciate the sense of community.

Remember, every person is an individual and everyone should be treated as such, as we all value different things. It's never advisable to judge the choices of others, but again if you are looking to make decisions to avoid potential problems, simply avoid what is statistically not safe.

Authorities advise to stay out of the conversations, the transactions, codes, colors, and cliques of gang life, *if* you care to go home on your earliest release date.

If you *are* interested in climbing a gang hierarchy, ask around for lessons and get involved. I'm sure you'll find something, as many gangs are usually open to recruiting new members. And when they question your motives, keep your answers open and honest.

Hopefully, you'll have no problems. It's unlikely, considering the top cause of violence in jail *is from* gang involvement, but like I said, *hopefully*.

IV. Drugs

If you care to go home, your best bet is to never get involved with drugs. No one will judge you for dabbling in your vice. However, if you choose to get high, it would be in your best interest to have all the necessary valuables to pay *upfront*. Pay for it, smoke it, and never worry about having a debt "in the street."

If you don't pay upfront, people *will* come to collect, and your name, reliability, and future dealings will be impacted. Any credibility developed thus far will be tarnished as well if you're the type of person to delay payment.

Further, your integrity could be impacted as the word about your mishaps travels throughout the facility. Be advised, that word travels very fast throughout prison as it is a close-knit environment.

Only you know if you're a procrastinator, so be advised it's better to have everything upfront so you'll never have to hear about it again.

To take it one step further, if you choose to pay at a later date, remember the people that collect will see just how easy it is for you to part with your belongings and that is unwise. Giving away your stuff is something you do not want to be doing or have anybody see you doing or else you will have frequent visits from people trying to exploit you. They will return again and again to constantly pressure you into giving away all your valuables.

A better alternative is to never open that door from the beginning. Countless people have started buying drugs and have become victims of extortion and are harassed as junkies. Masters of survival avoid the headache altogether and preemptively bypass a potential problem by never getting involved in the first place.

Lastly, consider you have purchased everything upfront and have no worries with the inmates. The correction officers take random urine tests and will lock you confined in the Special Housing Unit if you're found guilty of drug use. The jail administration deliberately gives severe consequences for drug infractions.

Violation of facility rules will not be tolerated so it's best to steer clear of violating them.

Veterans, me included, advise against drugs. But you're the one that has to make your own decisions, right?

V.Homosexual Involvement

In a community such as prison, homosexuality is socially unaccepted and shunned upon when members of the same sex are confined together.

Do not play any homo games, or have any homosexual involvement, unless of course, you are a homosexual. Comments are not perceived as shallow jokes like in society. Jail is a serious place and should be treated as such.

Now, of course there is nothing wrong with whatever your sexual orientation, so unless you are gay, don't act like it. Some inmates evaluate if you're coming out of the closet so it's best you stay clear with consistency about your orientation.

Further, jail partnerships come with domestic disputes that can get disorderly because of the emotional involvement. Some homosexual prisoners are the best fighters in the area, as several have fought all their lives. Many states have gay inmates that are notorious knockout artists that could potentially embarrass you once you're out cold. Staying away is a good option.

A. Rape Truth from National Inmate Survey (NIS)

The report below discusses state and county jails. The facts show that the numbers are low. These are *allegations* of misconduct, not convictions.

Jail is an environment full of rumors, where people *talk* nonsense, but the truth is, prison rape was more prevalent before the 1970's, not currently. Although the allegations and actions are very serious, if you follow the material outlined in this book, you won't have a concern on the issue of rape.

In prison, as in society, people will give you whatever you tolerate. If you accept being pushed around, you *will be* defiled. If you confront a violation, and stop any small offense *before* it escalates, the people around **have to** respect you if leave them no choice, right? It's not about what you deserve out of life. It's about what you **demand** from it.

N.I.S.

An estimated 4.4% of state prison inmates and 3.1% of county jail inmates reported experiencing one or more incidents of sexual victimization by another inmate or facility staff in the past 12 months or since admission to the facility, if less than 12 months. The report, Sexual Victimization Reported by Adult Correctional Authorities, 2007-2008, was released in January 2011. Among the report's findings: Administrators of adult correctional facilities reported 7,444 allegations of sexual victimization in 2008 and 7,374 allegations in 2007.

The number of allegations has risen since 2005, largely due to increases in prisons, where allegations increased 21% (from 4,791 in 2005 to 5,796 in 2008).

http://bjs.ojp.usdoj.gov/content/pub/pdf/pdca11.pdf

VI. Gambling

Authorities of prison consulting have opposing standpoints on this subject, but I advise *against* gambling, as most jails hold it in violation of the facility rules. Disciplinary infractions are reviewed when considered for release, and you're going to want a clean disciplinary record to increase your probability of going home.

If you choose to take a chance, then like anything else, make sure you have your gambling valuables upfront. Bring whatever you are wagering to the table, and only put them up for stake if you are prepared to lose them permanently.

Also, consider the prisoners there have been together for a long, long time and there are unions, politics, and rivalries way deeper than any amount of brownies you can offer. Sometimes, if you have extra supplies, it's better to simply trade off unwanted goods than to get involved with a prospective headache.

Some inmates work together and team up on unsuspecting players, especially new players to the tables. Some inmates cheat while others simply disregard the cheating, as to hustle you out of all your belongings. Inmates are patient and can hold off conversing about any shadiness until you walk away. You won't have any clue that you are sitting with corrupt players.

Also, there are many inmates that can do amazing card tricks, as they have learned legerdemain tactics. It is all too common for convicts to stack the cards in their favor, and against any odds of you ever winning, so it is in your best interest to evade the probable complication.

If you catch someone cheating, you are forced to confront them on it, and that can also turn into ugly violence. If you are trying to go home, stay away from the gambling tables. Don't get me wrong, it is possible to win an entire commissary bag. However, keep in mind it's a risk. Gambling is a risk.

Further, winning the entire tables' worth of commissary just might create some negative feelings with the inmates you're betting against, so beware, fights have occurred over the gambling tables throughout the history of man.

Again, it's all a gamble, and whatever you choose will determine just how high your stakes will be.

VII. Correctional Officers

In prison, you are not a person anymore. You are a number first and your humanity will be stripped upon entry. Guards and inmates alike will treat you with contempt, and sometimes disregard. You are wearing the same prison garb as every other inmate. It is best that you prepare now by accepting the guards are in control of *their* house.

All inmates share the same uniform and the guards treat all inmates the same, like scum. You can be a doctor in society and still be treated like the common thug in jail. The Correctional Officers are trained and hardened by their superiors to disregard compassion and treat you as if you are connected to a criminal enterprise.

It could be in the form of yelling at you for no apparent reason, excessively searching you for contraband, and humiliating you in front of your peers so make no mistake about it, the guards are top management and are there to babysit. They call the shots how they see fit and there isn't anyone to regulate their behavior, as they are all on the same team. Recording devices are not permitted inside jails and since the officers have the utmost responsibility, their word has an incredible amount of credibility. All other agencies of law enforcement, including the courts, will side with correctional staff because most actions are at the discretion of the administration.

It is common for Correctional Officers to bring their personal problems into work with them and take out their frustrations on the general population, so steer clear of agitating them. There is no one to monitor or regulate justice inside the prison.

Telling is more prevalent now than ever. Nobody likes a snitch, not even the correction officers, so honestly, don't be one.

If you need supplies, or have a basic procedural question, by all means, ask an officer, but *do not* get personal with the correctional staff. The C.O.'s are clearly there to uphold security and babysit, so do not get familiar at all, as *they will hurt you.*

If a situation ever arises and they have to choose between you and a fellow officer, you can be sure that you will go down fast. They will take the side of their colleagues, right or wrong.

They will write **you** a disciplinary sanction, confine you in a Special Housing Unit and it will go into your file permanently. This record gets reviewed by everyone that has any bearing on your treatment: Housing, Classification, Program Counselors, Possible Release Considerations, Time Allowance Committees, Furloughs, Parole Commissioner's, Correction Counselor's, etc. The documents are permanent and will be reviewed when discussing one of your seldom opportunities to go home, and the more sanctions you have, the less likely it is that you will be released.

You're going to want to maintain a clean disciplinary record, because once "the system" has its grips on you, it will *not* let go easily, sometimes never! Be vigilant about avoiding trouble. There is *no winning* against the C.O.'s, as you are in *their* house, so avoiding any unnecessary irritation is well worth the minimal effort you have put forth.

Veterans know *it is very* personal and not just business. Your tentative release affects your family, parents, partner, kids, career, health, and everything else that really matters. Think about it, and stay away from the guards, as they are not your friends.

Any reputable inmate would never get close with the officers, as it is a very clear line that should not be crossed. You will notice that officers sometimes abuse their authority and disrespect inmates so the less you are around them; the less likely you will be a target for their abuse.

It is best to avoid any problems and any dealings with the correctional staff, as you are simply trying to make your stay in prison as short as possible and go home on your earliest release date.

PART TWO: Advanced Methods

Standard Philosophies

The following section explains the wisdom of old school experts. The older generations lived by strict standards that have always worked throughout the history of prisons. Their methods and tactics are ancient, but combined with current generations; the modern strategies of today reap rewards for continuation and survival.

Respect

Respect is earned and not given away automatically. If you give respect to those around you, you will earn yourself the respect from others. It's not just in how you speak to people, but also in your ways and actions as well. For example, don't' stare people down with a mean face, trying to appear tough because it can be interpreted as you taunting others. Of course, maintaining an upset face *to yourself* is one thing because you are obviously upset in jail, and it's a defense mechanism, but "mean mugging" is clearly not keeping to yourself, it's an outward projection.

If someone is sleeping, respect their sacred slumber and politely keep your noise down to a minimum. If you are eating at a table, be courteous to the next person that may sit there by cleaning up after yourself. There are many ways to show consideration, and by consistently showing your words and behaviors are respectful, others will see it and give you the respect that you deserve.

Let Them Talk

One philosophy is, "Let people *say* whatever they wish. As long as they don't touch you or your property, pay them no mind." It's a basic jailhouse viewpoint and it is not always simple to follow. It takes understanding, patience, and self-control to realize that gossip has always been around since the history of man and it doesn't mean anything. This has helped countless inmates avoid problems because you're simply ignoring the beginning stages of an issue. There's only one person on your ID card. You came *into jail* alone and you will be *leaving* alone. The only person that matters is **you** so keep it that way, daily.

Don't Personalize a General Statement

Another core philosophy is, "They're not talking to *me*. Not like that. I'm going to assume they're not, as I'm too valuable of a person to just accept that kind of talk, so I'll ignore it."

This frame of mind permits you to ignore people as well as their negativity and ignorance. Some inmates say harsh things aloud about a given situation and as long as you don't personalize it, then you're not bothered by it. As long as they are only words, don't even acknowledge it.

Arrogance

This frame of mind sometimes gets confused with arrogance. I don't see it as pretentiousness, but if it gets perceived as such, that's okay. Besides, it's *perceived as* arrogance and nobody knows what's really on your mind, so it's okay to keep this mindset in full confidence and remain a mystery.

Further, for arguments sake, the *fact* is that you just don't respond to any type of energy that comes your way. This enables you to keep your focus on what you're doing and not be distracted by anyone else.

Remember, some prisoners *prefer* problems, so take notice, keep mental notes and keep it moving. You don't know all the details involved in everyone's business, and do not have all the answers. But definitely observe everyone, and everything, take mental notes, and you will quickly learn who is who, and what not to do.

If You Don't Know What To Do, Don't Do Anything

If you're ever in a situation whereas you are unsure what to do, *don't do anything*. When there are unknown variables, it's in your best interest to make time to think about any moves *before* you make them. You don't owe anybody anything and you don't have to make an irrational decision in the moment if you are not fully comfortable. A mistake can cost you consequences that far outweigh the benefits, so take some space and review all angles involved.

This is a great tool to step back and review your options and people will respect you for it. As a convict, stand your ground firm and explain you are unsure and need time to evaluate. If anyone doesn't respect that, maybe you should inquire why, because not allowing you time to think is suspicious.

I reiterate, when you don't know what to do, don't do anything. A lot of times, the best option will typically reveal itself. It usually does, so be patient, think and look for answers.

Influences

It's important you engage with positive inmates that are working towards self-correction. They, like you, are living everyday life working towards going home to stay for good. Being surrounded by like-minded people is the best way to ensure your goals, as you're likely to positively reinforce each other.

Focus on education, exercise and speaking positive as a general baseline. A balanced way of life is the best approach to just about anything, and if your standards are strict, people around you will notice, respect your focus, and will respond accordingly by giving you the space you need to improve yourself. In this way, you make it clear that you will not engage in other people's nonsense. This shows that you demand a high level of respect *from yourself* and *for yourself.*

If you socialize with ignorant people, you *will* be influenced into ignorance. Just as in chess: if you play with a weak player, your game becomes weaker. There is simply no way to avoid this and if you expose your thoughts to simplicity, you too will think in simplicity.

A commonality of all successful veterans is that they are always in tune to the messages they're feeding their brain. This is important for survival in prison as well as healthy successful living in general. Always take the time to surround yourself with healthy content whenever you can. It can be in the form of books, nutrition, building crafts, promoting life, and listening to positive messages. It will take some effort to notice the positive that surrounds you, but if you look for it, you will find it.

We can't control all the forces at work, but masters surround their brain with empowering material, and maybe you should too.

Standard Approaches

If You Act As a Victim

"If you act as a victim, you will become a victim." This is pretty straightforward and means how you go about approaching your everyday life is exactly the results you can expect. If you walk into a situation cowering and flinching, chances are someone will be aggressive towards you.

If you approach an issue with stability and fortitude, people will accept your confidence and might even sit back to learn your methods. How you approach any issue is how people interpret your character, so keep your composure in mind because everyone *is* watching.

Paralyzed Life is a Mistake

Masters of prison survival know that it is not a failure to be incarcerated. Everyone in this world has made plenty of mistakes and you just so happen to be in jail for your mistakes. It's normal to make errors in life and prison is only a temporary drawback. I cannot stress to you the importance of being focused. Get up, brush the blame and hurt off of you, and get back on that horse with courage! There are plenty of inmates that have a more unfortunate situation than you. Some prisoners injured innocent people through drunken accidents, some cannot read or write, and some convicts are so addicted to drugs they will use random chemicals until death separates them from each other. There have been mistakes and there have been virtues as well.

There's no getting around the fact that there are many people incarcerated with so much potential for greatness. What makes it worse is when people *accept* their shortcomings and are content to live as a blemished person.

It is *the acceptance of doing nothing about it* that is the true injustice. If you cannot read, that is ok; people will teach you if you ask. If you are handicapped, it is ok; people will help you if you allow them. There are millions of blemishes and deficiencies that are acceptable *as long as you are actively doing something to help change yourself.*

The self-defeatist mentality of accepting failure will keep you in your own mental prison. And the biggest thing to be without in this world is hope. So, take advantage of the time as much as possible and work on becoming the best at what you do. Focus on self-correction, as only **you can control** if you will be the next success story.

Be Leary of the Set Up

Learning from an experienced elder is the best opportunity to see the many facets of life inside a prison and another approach to consider before making a move is called "the set up." The following explains to you a possibility of what could happen in the prison environment.

A. The Set Up

'The set up' is a common trap played by veterans on new inmates just arriving in the housing location. Casually, one of your neighbors may ask you to pass a seemingly innocent bag of food over to your other neighbor. Beware, for if you do this, the receiving neighbor has the option of denying he ever got anything from you. There are no witnesses that could say one way or the other, so it's important to avoid passing items as a middle man, as one party may say he never received what the sender contributed. It gets especially interesting if there are irreplaceable valuables attached. This is a common trap for new inmates trying to be helpful and make friends. Guess who ends up footing the bill? You, so I advise against passing items that you're unsure about, as you can easily be the target of a set up.

Further, you could possibly be used as a drug mule and not even know it. It happens all too often on the new unsuspecting inmates. Avoid the unnecessary headaches as much as you can.

Charity

Charity in jail is not considered goodwill. Kindness often gets looked upon as a weakness, so if you *choose* to feed someone, or help out in some way, be clear about your commitment. The place is filled with ignorance and your kindness can develop into an expectation to give, as some people are prone to get demanding. Do you really *have to* give away your valuables to someone every single day?

A. Save Food for Night Time

The food you will receive in jail will be scarce, so it is a wise decision to save something off of every tray of the food offered to you. Hunger is common and if you save a small portion for yourself at night, it will be very satisfying.

Fights

There are many reasons for violence in jail and you are going to have to establish your personal boundaries. Other people and you will have to follow your limits so it is best to consider exactly the point in which you decide you are going to engage. Many people fear the unknown and having a fistfight in jail is as common as anything and once you realize there isn't anything to fear you will better mentally prepared.

Of course there are many reasons in which to avoid violence but there are times where you are forced to engage so let's so let's discuss a possible development.

First, if anyone touches you in any inappropriate manner you have to defend yourself. It is best you react quickly, and without fear as your first fight will usually set your standards. Fights can be scary and it is mostly more of a mental anguish than anything else. Besides, if it gets out of hand, the other inmates around will generally break it up if it's obvious one guy has had enough.

There are many variables to consider before a fight happens and there are many variables to consider as it is happening because the outcome is unpredictable. There is never a way to plan for a realistic result, and there is never really a way to plan a realistic introduction, as far too often, a fight hardly ever goes according to plan.

The main things to acknowledge are that it is hardly ever as bad as many people hype it up to be and once it's done, a fight is usually "not that bad." Some grow to enjoy the adrenaline and feelings of burning associated with a fistfight and realize a jailhouse fight is just that, no big deal.

Of course, there are a few cases in which things can get serious and this book outlines angles to consider. It should be noted that everyone has a different threshold for what they consider to be a violation and that's another factor why prison can sometimes be unstable. You can only control yourself with your own limitations and it's important to remember that because sometimes a difficult situation provokes you to question if the outcome is worth the input. It is mindful to you consider if you have crossed any boundaries, or if others have crossed any of yours because the bigger picture matters if you are trying to survive jail unscathed.

There are two main ways to engage in fighting. One is impulsive which is handling any infraction right there in the moment as it happens and the other is planning it.

A. Impulsive

The impulsive fight is the type that is usually for a minor discretion. Things such as verbal disrespect, arguing and other reasons as outlined in this guide increase the likelihood for an impulsive, spur of the moment encounter. This type holds the lowest chance of serious physical harm but holds the highest chance of getting into trouble with the correctional guards.

This is reckless because acting impulsively comes with an increased chance of getting caught by the correctional staff as this form of fight is usually out in the open and exposed to everyone around.

Obviously, getting caught by the C.O's is not what you want, as the consequences could be severe. Different states have different measures for violating the rules on fighting but one thing remains the same throughout all jails; once the guards catch you and yell for you to stop, you had better stop or else the guards will act with violence to stop you. They will spray you with pepper spray, hit you with batons, and lock you confined and neglected to "isolate the offender."

B. Planned

Planned bouts of violence have been notorious for causing the most physical harm because they are for the most serious violations. A planned encounter can result from many severe violations such as stealing, physical disrespect, drugs, gangs, and occasionally the inmate that has lived under such scrutiny, he cannot take anymore ridicule and snaps.

One never knows it is coming and the perpetrators use the element of surprise to cause serious injuries. Further, keep in mind some inmates never even know *why* it happened because they may never remember the infraction. There are some prisoners that are always up to something mischievous so it is best to always know who is who around you, and to carry yourself with respect so as to avoid any type of difficulty.

Planned violence is commonly undetected by the correctional staff until it is too late, after the brutality has already taken place. This heightens the chances of getting away with an attack because if nobody witnesses anything, nor testifies to seeing any wrong doing, then it is very difficult to hold anyone accountable.

Sometimes, in order to survive you are going to be forced into engaging in a fight as you need to defend your physical safety and protect yourself. "A coward dies a thousand deaths, but a soldier dies at once," is a common slogan for convicts because one single day of discomfort from a fight can open up the rest of your days for the troublemakers to leave you alone. With respect and dignity that you can be proud of, because you stood up for yourself and maintained your ground. You choices are your own, based on your value system.

You need to determine what is your level of tolerance and if you are disciplined enough to live by your own criteria daily. Make a decision about what your triggers will be, stay ready to act on them through the uncertain times. Aim to stand in full confidence so you have no regrets. Staying consistent teaches those around you, and if you change your ways, it gets noticed and you appear to either be unstable or show favoritism. For example, if a person of the same race as you makes a slightly inappropriate remark and you laugh it off while trying to engage in a fight with someone of a different race, you either appear to be favoring your race or inconsistent with your own beliefs. It is always better to stand firm, fair and consistent with your community as it shows those around you what are your limitations and boundaries.

Obviously, it is best to avoid any type of fight as it increases the likelihood of getting into trouble and may cause you to stay in prison longer. Remember to focus on your goal of going home daily, and you just may have the wherewithal and resources to get there sooner rather than later. "Keep your guard up and your head down" is a great maxim for new inmates, think about it.

Speed Tips*

* Prison is seniority ran. The inmates that call the shots have been incarcerated there the longest. The old timers have more authority in regards to TV, job functions, bottom bunk privileges, designated phone time, and other minor privileges as well. Simply respect your position if you're a new inmate in the housing unit. The power to control things will come to you in time.

* Always remember that your word is your bond, so don't lie and watch how you speak to others. "Walk in truth and you shall fear not." You are establishing integrity for yourself so choose carefully how you want to be distinguished because it is all on you. Carry yourself like a man, stand up for what's yours, and do what's right even when no one is watching, as integrity naturally attracts good company. You create how you deal with others. You dictate how others are to deal with you. This is an environment in which you start anew and you will make a name for yourself, for better or worse. If you want to go home, make good decisions with that ultimate goal in mind.

*There aren't any friends in here so this is the time to cut the cord, accept detachment, and trust in you. You will be okay. Remember, a bitter truth is better than a golden lie so always walk in truth.

*Prison is serious, and it can also be a way to forge the best qualities of a person. Understand, with neglect, you will be forced to be your own doctor. When hungry, you are forced to be your own chef. When your quarters are dirty, you become your own maid and so on. So be prepared to be your own spiritualist, mentor, your own guide, and the architect of your own life. Also, since your incarceration began, where are all your friends? Consider just how detached you are, and be your own best friend.

* The telephone is known as the "stress box." Use it with caution and be sure not to bother anyone else using the phone. You never know just how serious things are for the person standing right next to you. Whether it's because you're angry about being incarcerated, or you miss your family as they are out having pleasant times, talking on the phone is known to be very stressful. Some prefer to stay away altogether because of the heartache.

*Throughout your incarceration, be careful of creating the "idealized girl." Being incarcerated tends to form an abstract version of the people we love. Based on shared experiences with a past girlfriend, the natural process is to create a continued version of *that* girl. However, it may not be the real person anymore, so just be careful of your expectations, lest you set yourself up for resentment. If you decide to put energy into keeping relationships, try to discuss topics *in the present*. I've learned that when sharing current activities with one another, it breeds intimacy and a sense of togetherness.

Some inmates choose to immediately break ties with girlfriends, or assume they're moving on with their lives, to let go of the history. While in prison, it *is* history and focusing on what *she could be doing* can only bring you emotional distress. Stay away from it, as the stress is harmful.

Part Three: Why Life Is Not Over & How Time Away Can Be Beneficial

Psychology

There any many positive benefits to acknowledge when going away to a place where you will be alone most of the time. Jail is simply another chapter of your life and is not where people "end up."

Time is **perpetual** and you *will* end your term. What you achieve while there is completely up to you and within your control, so many inmates take advantage of the solitude and improve on the following areas of their lives.

Clean Time

A positive benefit of being incarcerated is the time abstained from all forms of toxins. Everything from drugs and alcohol to internet and fried foods are not available inside the prison walls and accumulating clean time will develop positive momentum.

For those that aren't associated with toxins, there are myriad distractions such as careers, women, material items and other factors that demand our attention. Under the seclusion and away from disease, distractions, or outside influences, it is now easier to focus on what's needed to survive this volatile environment. This privacy aids in understanding what's essential for clarity, self-preservation, and self-correction to keep moving forward.

Standing Alone

Independence is very important as incarceration forces you to become self-sufficient and competent to handle your own affairs. There is no family or any other aid to operate as a crutch and you are forced to grow into a fully separate, independent person of core strength to manage your dealings.

Integrity

In the jail environment, all anyone has is their word. The forced independence will make you realize how important it is to keep your integrity as a top priority. Your word is your bond, so when you make a commitment, it is best to keep it.

Integrity is critical when there are no materials and only your words bond the community together.

Furthermore, lying is a serious indiscretion and should be strictly avoided. If another inmate wants to live as a person with low values, let him, but the history of *your* character is shared as intelligence amongst the community. Too many transgressions or missteps and it's quite possible no one will ever vouch for you, or stop any harm from happening to you in the future. It's all too common to see the boy who cried wolf as abandoned and forsaken so keep your word sacred in all your affairs.

Inner Operations

Solitude is a great time to study and learn more about your inner mechanisms and is not the same thing as being alone or lonely. While you're away, learning more about yourself is a sure way to grow, strengthen and prepare for surviving whatever obstacle that may come your way. Prisoners are thrown into independence and a lot depends on *how* you look at it. What you make of it is up to you.

To understand what you think and *why* you think it is one of the greatest gifts that come with being incarcerated. The clarity that comes with knowledge of self builds confidence in your self-identity and helps you understand your place in the world.

Your Own Guide

Another advantage is the important freedom of being your own guide. Imprisoned, you need to make smart choices and keep the focus on what matters. You're going to have to be your own doctor because if you get sick, nobody will come running to help. If you get hungry, you are going to have to be your own cook. If you need comfort, you are going to have to provide what's best for you.

Neglect is common in jail, and from the tiniest details to the biggest challenges, you are ultimately on your own and you have the responsibility to be your own best keeper. Minding your own duties and staying focused on your goals will help ensure you achieve them.

Comfort and Esteem

An extra benefit of being self-sufficient is the comfort of knowing you are doing all you can to assist with the best outcome possible. By carrying yourself with honest integrity, and being your own best guide, you will be developing positive esteem and developing momentum in a constructive direction.

Self-esteem is a powerful emotion, as it encompasses the belief system and triumphs emotions such as despair, fear, and shame. These are all too common throughout today's prison system and boosting your esteem is a great way to build individuality and confidence.

Character

The jail environment forces you to become strong in character and offers to provide insight into the people around you. Being constantly encircled by the same people, you will be exposed to many different walks of life. It will be easier to quickly assess the character of other people as you get familiar with all different personality types.

Obviously, this makes deciding if you want to proceed with an alliance- or to abstain from dealing with any individual easier. Furthermore, an added benefit is once you are exposed to these systems in thinking, you will carry these skills for life.

Lastly, experiencing the different walks of life will make you more tolerant and will give you some insight into the different cultures, personalities and abilities of others.

Action

Conform to Rules

A peak ambition is that you can learn to conform to the rules in the jail environment. Following the rules can easily prevent any problems with the staff and ensure the probability of going home on your earliest release date. It is very easy to get into trouble and any disciplinary actions against you could easily discount any good time credits you may have achieved.

It's important to keep in mind that the correctional staff makes the consequences severe to show everyone that causing trouble will be costly. So, while imprisoned, make sure to follow the rules, as your goals will be contingent upon your ways and actions, and doing so will help you to be released back into society.

Learn a Trade

Many prisons throughout the country offer great programs for learning a trade and it is an opportunity to put your skills to use toward potential employment opportunities upon release. Furthermore, some states work in unison with the local

Department of Labor to credit you the full acclaim of your accomplishments.

Some states offer exclusive alternative to incarceration programs for those inmates that excel in their respective trade. There are many options to choose from and the best way to survive prison is to never be there. A work release program may be an option, so it may be important you take whatever opportunities are provided to you.

Many programs are put in place to increase your chances of going home, and also to enhance your employability potential upon release. Weigh your options and see if they help the bigger picture, getting you home quickly, and with a secure future. Be sure to inquire with your facility to review your best programming option.

Improve Work Ethic

Some states house correctional facilities that provide industry pay to inmates which is sufficient to survive comfortably on the inside, as well as the freedom to mail money home.

Sometimes, your security classification level demands your primary housing location to be in a disciplinary facility. These facilities are very strict and stress the importance of working long days, to instill a hard work ethic. These disciplinary facilities pay only pennies a day, and solely the real-life experience that comes with working a manual labor job.

Generally, you will have no choice in which type of facility you will be housed because security issues overrule all other factors. To find further details, inquire with the local facilities of your state to see what work programs are available, and what other options, if any, that will best suit your individual needs.

Learn to Read

Another great advantage of being away and on your own is the excessive amount of time you have to study. Countless inmates have learned to read, pursued an education, and have achieved college degrees.

"It is okay to be locked up, but it is a sin to do nothing to better yourself," is a common jailhouse slogan; studying is a great way to utilize the time of imprisonment and improve on any scholastic endeavors.

Prison libraries offer inmates the opportunity to not only peruse classic works of literature, but they also provide legal texts in law libraries for inmates to work on matters of law.

Exercise and Healthy Habits

One in three Americans are obese and going to jail is a sure way to eat only three meals a day. Prison will only provide you with three square meals a day, thus restricting overeating. Of course, food is available for purchase through the commissary and your dietary habits are at your discretion.

The survival secrets of veterans are to follow what's best for their bodies. Dieting and physical exercise are the mainstays of treatment for obesity and being overweight. Moreover, it is important to improve diet quality by reducing foods high in fat and sugars and by increasing the intake of dietary fiber.

Lastly, it's always in your best interest to find benefits that will help you survive in any volatile environment. Always remember, no matter what, life is constantly changing so if you are ever in a challenging state of mind, please find solace in knowing your incarceration will eventually end.

*There **are** good days ahead.* Stay optimistic and actively search for the good around you. It's there. Look for it.

Conclusion

By now, you should have a better understanding that prison life is not an easy way to live. The authorities allow the dynamics in prison to be how they've always been throughout history. It's **supposed to be** a messed up place. They were invented to be an unfair environment that you loathe, immediately and in the long term. Actually, if you think about it, jail is *exactly* how it's intended to be, treacherous and cruel. Thankfully, there has been an introduction of many methods, given away by masters, to deflect the traps and to avoid abuse within the prisons of today.

The above mentioned "Seven Secrets" are mostly negatives and throughout my research and recollection of past experiences, I've noticed it's more about restricting, and practicing self-restraint more than anything else. It's more about self-denial and accepting things as they are than it is about actually *doing* anything.

The best way to avoid of the bullshit...

...is to stay out of the bullshit.

It's clearly the negatives that will determine where you stand, what you value, and how you move towards where you're going.

I only hope you share the prison survival methods with younger generations that go through those cold prison walls. I believe those younger men and women should be educated to improve themselves through wisdom.

Occasionally, life may seem to ignore all your positive energy, and good deeds may sometimes appear to be wasted, but you can be sure the people that need your help are intensely searching for it.

Thank you for letting me contribute to your life in the hope of giving back a fraction of what was so kindly given to me; Love.

Keep your head up,

A Pisano

Thank you again for purchasing my book. As promised, I have more bonus material below.

In addition to my bonus books here, I have a special video that outlines the lessons in this book, more advanced lessons and stories. To gain access to this unique video, **please review my book on Amazon** and send me an email: prisonsurvivalsecrets@gmail.com. Once I confirm the review, I will send you a link to the bonus material.

Bonus Book #1: Prison Classifications

Security classifications of prisons consist of three main categories. It's important to know the differences between each type so you are aware of what to expect from each environment. You cannot get to a state correctional facility without going through a county jail first, so here is a breakdown of the different security classifications, their general requirements, and a common attitude of each. Although every individual facility is unique in its own settings, here is a guide for reference.

County Jails

County jails consist of recently incarcerated inmates. The county jail has the highest levels of frustration, as everyone is dealing with the sudden impact of being confined. People from all walks of life are mixed in together, are defending their cases, and have no idea what their outcomes will be. Inmates are missing their loved ones, detoxifying from drugs, and are hit with the sudden realization of the full impact of their crimes.

Common stories consist of girlfriends leaving, lawyers neglecting, and families that are detaching from the recidivist that has gotten into trouble again.

Generally, the county jail is designed to hold inmates for under a year, and this is the place where you will spend time before transferring to a state prison.

A. County Mentality

In county facilities, tension tends to escalate quickly, as there is no clarity with the majority of the ongoing criminal cases. With no light at the end of the tunnel, life is difficult to deal with for it is the unknown, the uncontrollable, that creates suffering. The county jail is a rough environment, and it may be best you keep to yourself.

Maximum Security State Correctional Facility

Once the central office of your state has made provisions for your transfer, a maximum correctional facility will generally be your destination to begin the reception process into the state prison system. Every state is different, but generally, only one religious book per inmate is permitted when transferring from the county jail into the state prison systems, and nothing more. Inmates generally use the blank pages to store all the personal information of their families, as well as contact people, for later use as an address book.

A. Reception

In reception, prison administration considers many factors to determine your security classification, and the location of your soon to be resident facility. They review the seriousness of the crime committed. Examples are: if there was violence involved, if it was a high profile case, victim injuries, prior criminal history, probation violations, and warrants amongst many other factors when deciding your individual program needs.

Every state has different priorities that will determine your classification status. A general baseline is if you are sentenced to serve seven years or more, you will likely be going to a maximum security state correctional facility as your "resident facility."

And just like anything else, there are benefits and limitations that come with your resident facility placement.

B. Max Mentality

A positive difference of a max prison is the inmates generally carry themselves with a much higher degree of respect for one another. The "lifers" or long-term bidders, have a way of carrying themselves that can only be described as pensive and deliberate. They have been incarcerated longer and know how quickly things can get barbaric. Considering just how dangerous this environment *could be*, most people don't want any trouble and are very clear to show respect for one another, as they are all around respectful of the environment in general.

Further, you're generally provided with more living space, although you will be locked in a cell longer than any other class of prison. You'll usually have your own cell for use as your own personal sanctuary. Your cell is going to be your home for the next few years and as long as you respect other peoples' boundaries, people will generally respect yours.

Lastly, many max prisons offer amenities that aim to alleviate any potential tension as well as attempt to make life bearable for the inmates that do follow the rules. Some maxes permit you to have a personal TV in your cell, as well as a hotpot for cooking, extra food/books, etc.*

* If you are soon going to prison, please note every facility in every state is different, and things are constantly changing, so it is recommend you contact the local facilities to inquire just what privileges are presently available. Connect with the "package room" of the facility and they will provide you with any information on allowable items. Do not assume you know anything even if you have prior experience, as there have been many recent changes in legislation and procedures. It would simply be a waste of your time to assume you know what's accepted, as it merely takes a phone call (or Internet search) to answer any questions you may have. Many clients that I have consulted are thankful, as the local package rooms have thanked them. Correctional staff accepts the inquiries, as it makes everyone's job easier. Any questions, call first, you'll be glad you did.

Medium Security State Correctional Facility

Medium facilities offer many more freedoms than max prisons, as they are usually a dormitory life. Commonly, you have to walk across the grounds to get from one building to the next for your programs throughout the day. The schools, jobs, recreation areas, libraries, and mess halls are all in different buildings, similar to a college campus. Of course, the correction officers determine when it's safe to move within the compound and they're always watching for any outbursts.

The medium security facility setting is considered a privilege and is where the majority of prisoners serve their time, as they represent the largest portion of the inmate population. But again, this depends on initial crime, years of commitment, degree of violence, program assessment needs, disciplinary history and many other factors as determined by the commissioner of your state.

A. Medium Mentality

The general attitude with the inmate population in medium facilities is that they are just naturally looser with how they interact with people, as many of the inmates are scheduled to go home in a few years (or less). It's easier to get comfortable with the other inmates and guards alike but the familiarity can sometimes cause problems as lines of respect get obscured. Things are different towards the ending of a sentence because you can now see the light at the end of the tunnel. That's why it's so important to set your standard boundary lines *early* and live by them.

Minimum Security State Correctional Facility

Minimum facilities are the final stages before being released, also known as "camps." This is the type of facility with the least amount of prisoners, and the most freedoms, as the staff knows your time is short, about a year or less. Usually, this is the class of facility that will offer inmates a working position with "outside clearance."

Working outside the confines of the facility can be beneficial if used in the right manner as you are preparing to go home. It's a good way to integrate with the transition by doing basic labor, such as local farm work, painting a church in the local town, porter and clerical work, and similar duties. Working outside the prison gates is viewed as one of the biggest privileges for any inmate, and the staff makes sure you earn your position on a daily basis.

The limitation in this setting is that it's easy to get into trouble here and potentially jeopardize any good behavior credits you've established throughout your incarceration. Countless others took advantage of the many freedoms offered, chanced unnecessary risks, and messed up the opportunity for others. Some inmates have attempted to have their associates stash drugs to be smuggled back inside the jail and some met up with old girlfriends for a quick romp, as inmates get arrogant and think that they're automatically going home on their projected release date. Some are natural risk-takers and fail to consider that the Department of Corrections has the final say in any impending release. Some neglect to consider that gambling with a government agency that has all their resources in trying to *keep* you and not wanting to release you, is not a wise risk to take.

The disciplinary sanctions imposed on anyone caught deviating and absconding are very severe. Many inmates have committed new felonies, been re-arrested, and spent years in solitary confinement behind the foolish decisions just mentioned.

Can you imagine explaining to your loved ones that you're not coming home on your earliest release date? Would you let your family know you're staying in prison longer because of a situation of which you took advantage?

The administration knows you are short to go home so they give you some slack in the hopes that you take the freedom seriously and do something constructive with time spent outside the confines of the facility. What you do with that freedom is up to you.

A. Minimum Mentality

The mentality in Camps is that inmates and guards alike test just how serious you are about going home.

Seasoned veterans know that the general attitude of the inmate population in minimum camps is the most difficult to endure because the majority of inmates are going home soon and are relaxed with their interactions.

The inmates provoke each other to mess-up and whoever allows himself to be agitated and act out is seen as really foolish. The price to pay for foolishness is staying incarcerated longer. The slang term for this is "Crash Dummy." People use Crash Dummies to antagonize and instigate problems. Whether it is for recreation, or to test the will of others, prison is a difficult way of life. As the saying goes: "the Devil loves company," and by being aware of it, you are a step ahead of it. With this clarity, you can act accordingly. Old timers dislike minimum camps because they know the counterfeit attitudes there would not be tolerated at all in max prisons, so some choose to refuse the transfer, if offered.

The officers get paid to monitor inmates, and it's *their* agency that determines if you're ready to be deemed fit for society. They are trained to look for inmates seriously looking to flourish if given a chance. And they quickly recognize the artificial inmates that just *say* they want to do well with freedom.

What would you do if you were due to be released from prison really soon? Would you wake up at first light, work hard labor all day on a farm, and be grateful if you were scheduled to return to your family, to an ex-girlfriend, within one month?

Minimum Camps know you ask yourself questions and they use it as a test. Maybe as leverage for cheap labor too, but ultimately, they know the choice is yours. You will determine how you consider the opportunity. Will it be a route towards achievement, or some way to be sneaky? Some "Lifers" will *never* have the opportunity. What will you do with yours?

It's always been your choice throughout life. What will you do with it?

Overall Mentality

You would *think* inmates are more prone to look out for one another so everyone can make it home quickly, but this is not true at all. Prison life has evolved throughout the years into something foreign that has never before been seen. Until the late 1970's, it *used to be* all inmates worked together to get out, *help each other get out, to stay out*. It is definitely not like that anymore. It's just how the natural process evolved itself.

It's important to take note that the overall education level within prison is far below the general population of society. It is assessed that the average education level throughout prisons is at an approximate eighth grade level. Consider this when questioning the mentality and value system of the average inmate, as sometimes it is best to "dumb it down" for the sake of maintaining harmony.

Differences in County and State

In general, the difference between county and state facilities is that state prisoners are afforded more freedoms and privileges. State facilities permit the smoking of cigarettes, better food, outdoor phones, longer visitations rights, bigger recreation yards with more activities available, better libraries, schools, and more.

Furthermore, state inmates have already been incarcerated for years, have accepted where they're at, and also know when they are to be released. This brings comfort to the anxiety that is prevalent in the county jails. State inmates are more accepting of other people as well, as they have been exposed to all different walks of life. The county inmates are not so forgiving.

So, in jail do what **you** need to do to get back to your loved ones. Take care of **yourself.** Avoid the pitfalls and take your time with whatever you choose to do; you have nothing but time, so use it and think before you act. Not many people will take the time to teach you the correct methods of surviving prison, and some will use your ignorance against you, but the references offered in this book help prevent that from happening. Use the information wisely to get back to the ones you love.

Bonus Book #2: The Inside Economy: What's Sacred, Traded and Sold.

Introduction

This is a guide to inform you just what's crucial in the economy of jail life. The following discusses the sacred items and shows you what is necessary to scale up and to be self-sufficient always. Many inmates learn to forever be self-competent, and as long as you have a small amount to invest, you can do it too. Humble beginnings breed momentum so you can take the framework, learn these principals, and apply them for life. Providing for you is worth its weight in gold.

Sacred Items

There are many sacred items in jail. Every housing location is different throughout the state, but here is a basic listing of common sacred objects:

An inmate's cell is his sanctum. If you are ever invited into someone's cell, do not touch anything. Furthermore, do not sit on someone else's bed. Many years ago, it used to imply a gay communion and that's not the impression you want to project when you're simply trying to sit down. Besides, you shouldn't be that comfortable with anyone to be sitting on their bed.

More importantly, the pillow is a sacred item as well. Do not touch it, and don't permit anyone to touch yours. You have to put your face on it and its part of the very few personal belongings you have.

Food is considered sacred as well. Food sent from home is especially important because it may be the only love from society that's sent into the facility. Don't ever play with another inmate's food, as that is a sure way to start a problem.

Mail and photos may be the only items to represent freedom that the prisoners have to hold on to, so don't play with anyone's photos and mail because they are very personal objects too.

All religious books are sacred as well. Consider this is has an extra level of sacredness because the book could potentially have the addresses of an inmate's contact people. Only one religious book per inmate is permitted when transferring from the county jail into the state prison system. Since these books have all the personal information of the inmate's contact people, do not touch what's not yours. Even if asked to briefly pass it, explain you don't get that comfortable with people and any convict that has been around awhile will understand you limit your level of involvement with people as well as minimize the risks you take. It's completely understandable to err on the side of keeping a safe distance, and in fact it's usually the best bet, especially with the sensitive information of this kind.

Economy Inside

I am asked often about the objects of value in jail. There is no cash so let's discuss the economy.

The same rules apply *inside* prisons that apply in society. It is important you **make your offer before** you ask for what you want. It is all too common for beggars to constantly ask for goods, so the best way to avoid being denied as a beggar is to *offer* something first.

With minimal materials to offer, the best starting point is to use humor. If you can make an inmate laugh before you make your proposition, you will begin in a good starting position. If you can make someone laugh, or dispel stress, then inmates will likely warmly welcome your friendship and business.

Further, don't be a complainer while trying to trade goods. Complainers are weak and if you look around **everyone** has problems. Focus on how to benefit the person you are dealing with first then discuss you afterwards. If you are the one with an optimistic attitude, you'll be sought as much easier to work with and welcomed.

Lastly, don't ask for anything unless you *really* need the help. Learn to be self-sufficient, or learn to do without.

Currency

The most valuable items are as follows and in this order, respectively: Stamps, cigarettes, coffee, food (meats and cheeses), snacks (cakes and pies), music, porno magazines, and clothing.

Remember, everyone values different things at different times. A non-smoker might value stamps in the immediate, but will benefit from the porno magazine at a later time, but basically, stamps, cigarettes, and coffee dominate the trade market. Next it's food, then entertainment, then clothing. In conclusion, it's best to have somewhat of an understanding of what's valuable to that person before negotiating with your potential affiliate.

Tips and Methods

There are many ways to handle your valuables on the inside and one is called "Juggling." Juggling is as old as jail itself and occurs when you loan out an item to have two returned back. The person you're dealing with brings you back two items, because he borrowed it when he didn't have it available. So, for making you wait until he can get it back, you double your money as payment.

People generally borrow food items, as food is necessary to eat and is easily replaceable. It could come in the form of a box of pancake mix or a box of chicken. If you already have three boxes of pancake mix, why let it sit? It could be juggled out to return profits to you. It is always better to have your investment out there making money than it is just sitting in your locker. Obviously, it's advisable to keep your risks small so if anyone transfers out, or doesn't pay, you stand the chance of losing next to nothing.

Sometimes it's better if someone refuses to pay you so you never have to deal with that shady person again. If a person were to burn you on a small item such as pancake mix, then it's in your best interest to not have that caliber of person around you. Think about it.

If you are going to have your assets work for you, always trade towards something more valuable to scale up. Moving up the currency chain is beneficial because you can literally acquire some real quality goods from what was essentially nothing form the beginning.

An example of this is getting ten postage stamps for giving someone a haircut. A week later, an inmate asks you to borrow 10 stamps so he can try his luck with gambling. You give it to him for 20 in return, and no matter if he wins or loses, you want your 20 on payday. Okay. After you receive the 20 stamps, you buy a pack of cigarettes and wait until a smoker is desperate and without cigarettes. This may take a week or even two, but it's worth it. Many smokers need the tobacco and will gladly give you two packs later in return for one now. Especially, if they are awaiting a carton that will come in a few days, they will be delighted. Lastly, with these two new packs, you can simply trade them up to someone for a nice dress sweater. And this sweater will last way longer than any haircut, stamp, and tobacco product.

This was only one of the many methods you can try while there. And if you're known as one who makes arrangements in bartering, some great items will just naturally come to you. This is totally legal so enjoy your profits and may you remember the tactics always.

Conclusion

Remember, different people like different things at different times and you can always find an opportunity, just like you can always find optimism. The important thing is you are going to have to actively look for it first. With a little work invested, you can set it up where your locker is always full of food, and money always being dropped off by other inmates bringing you their full commissary bags every week. You get really good when you are giving away the old stuff to keep it from getting spoiled and trashed. That's when you know you are eating well and that, my friend, is also called optimism. Take advantage of it.

Bonus Book #3: True Stories of Trial and Error

"Let people say whatever they wish, as long as they don't touch you or your property, then pay them no mind."

This is not always easy to follow. Here are two true stories showing just how difficult it can be to clearly define the rules of engagement. The rules of jail dictate one way to proceed; however, circumstances are not always so clean cut and the advice not so easy to accept.

One is the story of a guy that *didn't touch* me or my property; however, I wanted to fight him anyway. The other is of an inmate that *did* in fact steal from me but maybe I was wrong for engaging in violence.

It is **very** *advisable* to not put yourself in a lose/lose situation. But like I said earlier, "countless trial and errors," so do not repeat what you are about to read, as some mistakes are embarrassing.

Bad Gamble

I was in county jail when a new inmate came into the dorm. His first day there, I was sitting at the chess tables playing chess as I normally did back then. This new inmate stood around quietly observing the ongoing games taking place and looked for his inlet to play a competitor. For a few days, he watched and didn't say much to anyone.

A few days later, it wasn't until I played my last move against an opponent did the new guy call to play the next game. He sat, we briefly introduced ourselves and we played chess for a few hours. Hours came and went and the games turned into an all evening event. Chess became an everyday thing because, well, this guy was pretty good.

That was how I met, Sha.

About a week later, Sha and I were sitting by the T.V. and a commercial came on that mentioned the word "totalitarianism." I immediately said to my chess nemesis, "There is no such word as that." I had been doing a lot of writing at that time, studying words and such, and didn't remember ever seeing a word like that.

So, Mr. Chess Master chimes in with "yes, there is." Now, being that I was comfortable in the dorm, and also with the people around, I foolishly said "If that is a valid word I will give you everything I own." As I put out my hand, he immediately shook it and the bet was sealed. Naturally, we went back to my cell to check the dictionary.

I was shocked!! I was so dead wrong. He was right! What was I going to do? I just bet away everything I owned!

Thereafter, for days I was hounded about the bet with comments such as "oh, you're wearing *my* shirt today." or "those are nice magazines. Are they *my* Maxim's?" "Who are you writing, *my* girl?"

After a while, I got angry and didn't know what to do. The guy was right. I opened the door by betting on something I had no idea about, and now I owe him. My word is my bond, right?

After stalling for as long as I could, I initially paid him with some magazines and cupcakes and random goods of non-importance. But sure enough, once he ate them, he came back for more and now I seemed to have a real issue on my hands. But what was I going to do? I invited this.

Shortly thereafter, he made an inappropriate comment and I couldn't take it anymore. I was so angry and confused I figured if I were to scare him, it would make him leave me alone and squash the debt. So I invited him into an open cell to fight discreetly.

He didn't show up for the brawl. He didn't enter that cell so there I was, standing alone and mistaken because I chose to foolishly speak when I should have just enjoyed some stupid commercial. Also, wanting to physically pummel this guy who did no wrong is even worse because he didn't provoke the bet, *I did!*

I was wrong on many levels and broke out of the many standards of jail. Further, the more I thought about it, the more I realized that no matter the route I chose I would have been wrong. I should have never opened my mouth.

Let's review:

On the one hand, I was not going to lose my credibility in the dorm by becoming a liar and a bully. My word is my bond and I take it seriously and I am not one to be into abuse so I had no intention of living as a bully.

But on the other hand, I wasn't going to just give away all my belongings, either. It took me eleven months to gather all that I had, so what was I going to do? Just give away 11 months to some new guy? Me and my big mouth.

I went to my cell to lie down to think for the night. While contemplating, I fell asleep.

The next morning, as the food was being distributed, I got a lucky break. The guards call Mr. Chess Master over the loud speaker telling him to get dressed and ready for court. So, considering Sha will be gone for at least the next few hours, I discussed my current dilemma with a close associate for advice.

Around 3 pm, the court trip was being returned and a mutual associate comes to me while I was playing chess. He gives me the news that Sha, the chess master, got his bail reduced and went home immediately after court.

I was so relieved. I was fortunate for his leaving because I clearly made many mistakes. At that time, I was young and naïve and my dealings with Sha definitely left an impression on me. The lessons were important and I will remember them always.

Don't foolishly gamble on the *unknown*.

1. Don't pursue fighting with anyone that did nothing to harm me.

2. Defending myself would have been one thing, but that was clearly not self-defense.

The truth of the matter is that I was too comfortable and unwise during that time. It would have better if I had never opened the door to begin with, as I was ignorant and inexperienced. And although I'm accountable for all my actions, I would have been tremendously grateful had I been taught the effective rules of prison prior to making errors. If I was better prepared, I could have avoided many mistakes and would have adapted better.

I disclose my mistakes because I believe they will teach how *not* to carry yourself while imprisoned. I just happened to get lucky that day. Who knows? **Your** Sha may not ever get bailed out.

To Catch a Thief

During a completely different period, in a different dormitory, there was an inmate that transferred into my housing location. I noticed him as a new face, but thought nothing of him, as people frequently come and go in jail.

After he was in the dorm a few days, we played basketball together in the recreation yard. He seemed like a regular local, as the common personality type is an aspiring gangster, so it was easy to assume this guy was normal.

After the yard, naturally, I gathered my soap and towel and headed toward the showers. When putting up my towel, my neighbor tells me "Hey, Pisano, someone just walked into your cell".

Without hesitation, I grabbed my towel and left the shower area to investigate my living quarters, as it is my sanctuary. I looked in and witnessed the new guy standing near my bed holding what appeared to be my Walkman. I never even got his name and as I step inside my temporary home, I politely ask him to hand me the

Walkman. He reached out to me as I gently took it out of his hands, confirmed it was mine, and placed it nicely on the bed.

I quickly processed he was about 50 pounds lighter than me and not in as good physical condition as me. I caught him red handed stealing from my sacred living quarters and the rules of jail mandate something had to be done. I couldn't let this slide, or I would've easily become a target myself. Inmates would interpret this as cowardice and very quickly they will come to reign their abuse.

I caught him with my Walkman in his hand and although I didn't want to fight this dude, *I had to*. He broke the rules of the land, and it's something we all must do in that situation. Win or lose I had to swing and that's exactly what I did. I fiercely pummeled this violator with swift punches to his face and body until he managed to get around me and escape the cell.

After he got his lumps, I quickly went back to the showers as the guards will quickly lock everyone in their cells if they're alarmed of a fight, and I was not going to skip my shower.

The "A man," who basically ran the dorm, took notice of what had just transpired, and before any further incidents, he had the correctional officers lock the thief in his cell for his own protection. The rest of the prisoners in the dorm would not have tolerated a sneak thief living amongst us. Everyone would have abused and ridiculed him for trying to be sneaky like that and it was clear they would've really hurt this dude.

Confronting a person in their presence and aggressively take something is one thing, but to be a sneak thief is not acceptable.

All ended quietly and for the rest of the night the violator was locked inside his cell.

As the next few days pressed on, he never left his cell and I noticed his state was peculiar to me. He would whisper to someone not present, pour powder all over himself, rip papers into tiny pieces and pour them over his head, rock back and forth, and would just act a bit imbalanced overall.

I noticed this and felt bad that I had to beat up someone with what appeared to be mental problems. I am no bully, but what was I supposed to do? I didn't know he had a handicap and I found him in my cell stealing from me.

Nobody should have to tolerate stealing, and in prison everyone has to sometimes make tough decisions to survive, and although I felt bad about what I learned *after* the fact, it was just one of those times I had to do what was expected of anyone in that moment.

Final Thought

Imprisoned, there are tough rules to live by, and if I didn't act in those situations, I would have become a bull's-eye to be tormented and annoyed everyday thereafter. I myself would have become a victim if I didn't act, and although radical, under those conditions, it's expected for anyone's life to get harsh.

The situations were for you to see just how difficult life can be behind bars and although the circumstances aren't always easy to define, with education, clarity and guidance, we all can be better equipped to handle any anomaly that comes our way. I aspired to provide useful tools for you.

There are people that won't teach the true survival methods, and I aim to reveal exactly what's necessary to survive while incarcerated because I believe in preparation, and being ready as the best approach to any situation.

That is what I believe and that was the purpose of this book.

About the Author

A Pisano is a prison expert, with a focus on prison preparation and new inmate consulting. The author has over ten years' experience in prison and dealing with inmates. His website, http://www.prisonsurvivalsecrets.com provides resources for soon to be inmates, and their families alike. His published work has helped numerous people prepare for the transitions associated with going to prison. He advises, "The situation *is* unfortunate, and there's *no* getting around it. But you don't have to be helpless. You can be in control every single day." You can also find more of his material online @ prisonsurvivalsecrets.com.

Thank you, I have a special video that outlines the lessons in this book, more advanced lessons and stories. To gain access to this unique video, **please review my book on Amazon** and send me an email at prisonsurvivalsecrets@gmail.com. Once I confirm the review, I will send you a link to the bonus material.

Thank you again for purchasing my Book.

Made in the USA
San Bernardino, CA
20 January 2014